William Sharpe

The conqueror's dream

And other poems

William Sharpe

The conqueror's dream
And other poems

ISBN/EAN: 9783743313361

Manufactured in Europe, USA, Canada, Australia, Japa

Cover: Foto ©ninafisch / pixelio.de

Manufactured and distributed by brebook publishing software (www.brebook.com)

William Sharpe

The conqueror's dream

THE CONQUEROR'S DREAM

AND

OTHER POEMS

BY

WILLIAM SHARPE, M.D

AUTHOR OF "HUMANITY AND THE MAN" ETC

NEW EDITION REVISED

NEW YORK
G. P. PUTNAM'S SONS
182 FIFTH AVENUE
1881

For in proportion to his innate worth,
His love of truth and sense of right and wrong
Shall he precedence take and overcome ;
For nature still the higher calls to rule
And to that end are they endowed by her
With courage, strength, and intellectual power.
—*Humanity and the Man.*

CONTENTS.

	PAGE
THE CONQUEROR'S DREAM............................	1
THE PALM GROVES (Parel)...........................	26
THE SOLDIERS' CEMETERY (Khandalla)................	36
THE WARBLER AND THE BIRD-COLLECTOR...............	39
THE EYRIE ON THE SEA-CLIFF........................	50
THE HEIGHTS OF KHANDALLA.........................	63

THE CONQUEROR'S DREAM.

ERE yet ambition's tempting heights he scaled,
In vision strange the youthful warrior saw
An outline of his future destiny
Linked with the semblance a mighty hall
That far surpassed and dwarfed the works of man.
'Twas thus unfolded to his wondering gaze.

An edifice, vague, undefined, and vast,
Stupendous rose high as a mountain range.
One central tower o'erlooked the mighty pile,
And Babel-like in middle air shot high,
Seeming to pierce and vanish in the clouds.
Disclosed around the open portals stood,
And over them the girding arches frowned,

Gigantic there on fluted columns raised.
On either side was moving to and fro
A motley crowd that ever seemed to pass
And repass through the gates innumerable,
Which led remote by winding corridors
Unto the courts that lay beneath the dome.
The warrior also entered with the throng,
Anxious to see, but not like them content
The central portions of the hall to find;
He longed, instead, the topmost height to gain,
And thence the wide extended tracts survey,
Of hill and dale and wood and fertile plain.

Anon the din of tongues confused and loud
And clashing sounds on either side arise,
Discordant, grating on his ears, till now,
But ill accustomed to the rude turmoil.
Here much perplexed, through labyrinthine courts
At large he strayed, unnoticed and unknown,

THE CONQUEROR'S DREAM.

Seeking, indeed if haply he might find,
Some flight or stair by which he might ascend.
Desponding, and uncertain which to choose,
Now this, now that, with persevering toil,
In vain he tries, still foiled in the attempt,
Till, with the labor well-nigh overcome,
He paused, and much debated with himself
What course he should adopt ere finally
He would resolve to quit the fruitless task.

But now, as 'mong the multitude he passed,
An ancient warden of the place he found,
And him he importuned to point the way
Which led unto the summit of the tower.
At first dissuading much the old man spake,
Forbidding him the rash emprise to tempt.
But seeing him by words unmoved and still
The more inclined the arduous task to try,
Through many a hall and winding maze he led

To where the stairs their tortuous course began.

Ascending thence, an open space they gained,

Whence rose the dome and tower's enormous pile.

But here, in front the frowning ramparts rise;

And towering bastions and jutting tiers

Of adamant the main approach command,

And tranverse beams and studded gates of brass

The archway and the gloomy entrance bar.

Helpless he gazed and thought on his return,

When straight his guide, more confident, advanced

And with a touch the jarring bolts undid:

And lo! anon the ponderous doors revolve,

Till open wide the brazen portals lay.

Once more the aged and venerable sage

The ardent youth advised, the while he spake

Pity and sadness mingled on his brow.

"Here now, of guide," he said, "my office ends,

From this thou must ascend alone, but well

Bethink thee of the dangers to be passed,
And toil immense, beyond thy utmost strength.
Or shouldest thou by fate or chance attain
The giddy summit of yon cloud-capped tower
That high in air terrific frowns, impendent,
Threatening chaotic ruin, such as marked
The fall, ere now, of Chimborazo's peaks,
When from their rocky basis hurled amain,
With savage din they tossed into the gulf
That yawned beneath them like a molten sea,
Far other sight, I warrant thee, than that,
Of which, indeed, thou fondly dreamest now,
Will sudden meet thy much astonished gaze."
This said, the old man pressed his hand and bowed,
Then slowly sought the basement of the hall.

The warrior now with confidence restored
His upward way resumed, nor did he hence
Obstruction or impeding hindrance meet,

Till high 'bove turrets, domes and battlements
He stood in front the steep ascent which scaled,
The central tower. Below unequal stand
The lesser heights as in some alpine range
The lesser peaks, unequal group around
Some mighty cone that rears above the clouds
Its snow-crowned head, immense in upper air

But here balked in th' attempt to scale the tower
And by the aspect of the course deterred
An eager crowd the narrow way obstructs;
In vain dispute contending 'mong themselves
As to the means whereby they might ascend.
Yet each in turn drew back, none would be first,
Or risk the danger that seemed imminent,
But fain would be supported by the others.
Aside to right and left the impetuous youth
Unheeding thrust the noisy throng as straight
Unto the narrow stair he forced his way.

THE CONQUEROR'S DREAM.

Sheer up the perpendicular steps he sped,
As there aloft in open space they rose,
Unto the square or landing on the tower.
No guard was seen or bannister to nerve
The giddy brain, but one small rope, like lure
Of seeming strength, the daring wight to tempt
To the ascent, which, if his hold he lose,
Like rope of sand or brittle thread disjoins.

Hardly had he, the dizzy summit gained
When lo! a spectacle disclosed itself
That filled his soul with horror and dismay;
For there beneath the lowering heavens exposed
Upon a circular platform on the tower,
A ghastly group, by wasting famine pinched,
Astounds the sense ; on divers couches they
Reclined, mere skeletons, all but extinct,
Their shrivelled features and their hollow eyes
In contrast strange to robes of regal dye,

With ermine trimmed and gold. A few still moved,
But seemed oppressed by cares unbearable.
Aghast the warrior stood ; thrill after thrill
Of horror shot across his 'wildered brain ;
As on some stormy coast wave after wave
Impetuous drives, commingling with the sands,
Till all the beach is strewn with heaps of foam.
Then turning round instinctively he called
To those below, imploring them to find
Some stimulant that might afford relief
Till aid should come. In vain he called and called,
None came or heard or, hearing, heeded not.
Distract for aid, he must himself descend.
But now was still more horrified to find
Descent impossible ; the way was barred ;
A pond'rous door had swung into its place
And with the clash its brazen bolts were fixed.
Perplexed he stood uncertain how to act,
When lo ! from off his gold-embroidered couch

THE CONQUEROR'S DREAM.

One of the seeming invalids arose,
Walking erect with ease and dignity;
And thus to him the mystery unfolds,
Speaking the while in accents of command
With words and tone that thrilled his inmost soul.

"Thou seest this mighty pile with domes and
towers
And pinnacles and battlements outspread.
Collectively it represents the sum
Of human progress and the utmost span
Attained by civilization; and this height
Whereon thou standest now, is rightly named
Ambition's tower, the point which binds, commands
And stays the whole, like keystone in the arch,
Yet not like it in keeping fair, compact,
The seal and token of the finished work,
But rude, unequal, disproportioned, vast,
Yet seeming here the best that can be had.

THE CONQUEROR'S DREAM.

"With thoughtless haste, resistless you have scaled,
The tower, and found a bubble on the top,
Whose gaudy colors, like the rainbow, lured
At distance with its unsubstantial show.
There is thy niche! repose thee there as best
Thou canst, till famine waste thee to the core!
Yet know, 'tis famine of the mind,—a want,
Of human sympathy; far from thy kind
Removed, thou shalt instead have outward show,
'Mouth honor' coldly tendered from afar,
With awful reverence and ceremony.
E'en flattery shall now more odious grow,
More base and hollow, clad in double robes
Of darkest hypocrisy. Begirt with all
The guady trappery of wealth and power
And seeming luxury thou'lt starve outright!

"Thou would'st descend? Ay, if thou could'st;
  too late!

That cord that drew thee up, ambition's cord,
Will never serve to let thee down ; yet more,
Come, see the steps by which thou did'st ascend :
Come witness here a sight to strike thee dumb :
Behold them clotted o'er with human blood !
And hideous raised on piles of human bones !
And see beyond—thy work upon the plain !—
Those mangled carcasses and heaps of dead
On which the wolves and carrion vultures prey !
How fair the vision from this cloud-capped tower !
What ! is the prospect now to be admired ?
Hearest thou that cry ? that cry that rends the air !
The homeless orphan's and the widow's cry !
The wail combined of anguish and despair !
Seest thou their tears ! Wilt join them in their woe !
With them weep drops of blood ? Thou hast good
       cause.
Descend and mourn and act the comforter.
Think'st thou they will appreciate thy grief ?

Will't heal their wounds? Will't call the dead to life?
Descend, and further blast them with thy sight!
Descend, and they will strangle thee outright!
Though here they will extol thee as a god!
Descend indeed! never! here must thou bide
Till time release or fate dispatch thee hence
To mingle with the nameless dead, whose bones
Are whitening on the desert plain, where late
With haughty head and stern unchanging brow
Thou rodest in blood and, foremost in the van
Thy voice above the din of war was heard.

" Yet comfort thee somewhat, if that thou canst,
For know, thou'rt but an agent in the fray.
Though dark and terrible, all's not so dark
As now it seems, that is, compared with what
It would have been if no one did ascend:
These towers must still be manned, so fate ordains,
At least till the Millennium comes—blessed time!

If come indeed it ever shall ; if this
Be not rather a place where all are tried
In some degree, and by experience taught,
As preparation meet for some higher sphere,
If fame speak true, than this our ball of earth.
No sign as yet of much amendment here,
Or better world than this we now possess,
Whate'er it be ; but this we know, that we
Are called to act, and exercise the will,
In balancing affairs, where 'tis ordained
That good and evil ever shall contend
For mastery, waging eternal strife!

"See imperfections everywhere abound.
Huge disproportions mark this edifice
In all its parts, with all the thousand ills
Concomitant thereto. This is not good;
But think, is it according to desert?
Apportioned just ; the best we can obtain ?

For higher state man seems as yet unfit
As he has oft to demonstration proved.
E'en this now reached, he hardly can retain.

"Thou did'st ascend, 'tis true, o'er heaps of dead,
Not good! but of two evils much the less.
For better this, appalling as it seems,
Than that the whole of this vast edifice,
Our safety here and stay 'gainst greater ills,
In hideous fall and ruin be involved,
O'erthrown by yon insensate multitude
In their infernal rage. They on themselves,
Unless restrained by force of iron will,
Would carnage foul and dire destruction bring.
Better by far that many weep, as now,
Than that none should be left to weep at all.

"On every side, what countless ills exist!
Here ghastly stride the many shapes of death!

Here destitution wan, and penury,
With all their doleful train—wasting disease,
Repellent squalor, wretchedness and crime.
Here boundless Wealth, hungry as death, engulfs
In his capacious maw the sustenance
Of toiling millions, dealing out his dole
The while with niggard hand to poverty;
With mighty fuss doct'ring the sore he fain
Would hide with irritant that more inflames.
Enough of toil, to make the desert like
A garden teem, is unproductive spent
His every whim or wish to gratify.
O'er all earth's wares he holds monopoly;
Now gold unlimited and now the law
He wields, his tool subservient to his will,
A chancery confused, where talk runs riot,
A tangled maze, where hobbled justice creeps
With faltering step, too slow to reach the poor.

" These, the chief lures, the horrid idol flaunts
Unblushingly to tempt his votaries
To bow before his shrine, to offer there
Truth, honor, justice and humanity,
The treasures of the soul beyond all price;
That he may freely give them gold instead,
Wherewith his gewgaws to command. Gold! gold!
For this the earth with violence is filled,
Corruption stalks like pestilence abroad
Bearing the stamp of mammon on his brow,
The hateful brand of meagre selfishness.
Through city, hamlet, castle, cot he strides,
Tainting with plague more fell, more fatal far
Than ever sprang from Egypt's steaming plains!
Through church and state the deadly poison spreads;
E'en commerce groans, infected to the core,
Commerce, great foster mother of mankind,
That closer drew the bonds of brotherhood,
And in the van of human progress led.

"For gold, nation with nation, man with man
Still strive in contest fierce, struggling that each
Unto themselves a double share may wrest.
The hideous idol, they, like those of old,
In many ways with blood propitiate ;
Now openly, whole hecatombs they slay ;
And now, like Thug, their victim they seduce
With seeming friendship and with hollow show
Of proffered good the while they dig his grave

"Such are the ills in part thou must restrain
And keep in bounds with stroke of iron rod.
Now, as in days before the flood, they bear
Within themselves the seeds of anarchy.
They are the harbingers, now as of yore,
Of mental lapse and movements retrograde :
Nor did the words of Noah much avail
Man's downward course to stay ; for each and all
Bore in themselves the subtle taint of death ;

Came then, as now, under extinction's curse!

Humanity may grieve for this the doom,

That ever in the wake of evil drives;

But not for this will nature change in aught

Or e'er reverse the sequence of her law

Which, seeming harsh, is in the issue kind.

Of evil omen truly is the sign

When knavish cunning blurs the intellect

And simple truth and honesty are fled.

No constitutional palladiums try,

When nations come to grovelling pass like this:

Decrees alone peremptorily enforced,

Not words and soothing arguments, well framed

To guide and to persuade, will then avail

To stay the malady incurable,

That cancer-like insidious infiltrates

Through every nerve to civilization's core.

This truth of primal import, ever thou

Must bear in mind, not trusting doctrines vague,

Endless propounded to the multitude
With much parade, though all to none effect:
Fine sentiments concerning equal rights
Where each by fraud would the advantage hold
And monsters prey-like fishes on their kind,
Though not like fishes unprovided else;
And men's equality that's nowhere seen
Save in the pages of Comtean lore.
Wild schemes at best of doubtful efficacy,
Delusions vain, fair arguments on false
Foundations based, to wit, that evil may
Be reasoned with, persuaded to be good!
As soon believe that leopards change their skin!
Nor think that man shall much assistance find
To right his course in statutes, precepts, acts
And divers rulings endless multiplied,
As now they stand, pile set on pile, confused,
A dreary waste of truth entangling words,
Where simple justice helpless·lies enmeshed.

And juggling knaves upon their victims prey
At will, secure, eluding all pursuit
When danger nears by hiding in their dens,
Ensconced behind their inkbags and their scrolls,
Like octopods hard by their ocean caves,
That now a thousand hungry suckers ply
And now, alarmed, their grumous jet discharge
Till all the crystal element is dyed.
Trust not this wilderness of words called law;
For see the crazy world now how it tugs
And on its laboring axle groans and creaks
Despite the laws and pleas and recipes
Like grease applied, the friction screams to drown.
Sweep all such fusty rubbish from thy path:
Build up a new and simple code of laws
Or fail, like us in patching up the old
With purblind legal pedants for your guides,
With one result, that knavery shall thrive,
And swarming harpies with impunity

Shall in the sacred name of justice rob,
And with their baseness taint the minds of men
Till lowest cunning ousts the intellect
And all the nation suffers from the change.
Nor trust political economies.
Philosophies in theory far famed!
Behold the accompaniments! where will they end?
Where end those ever-growing monuments?
That rise to destitution and disease,
To lunacy and crime, grim ominous,
As if in 'mockery of man's progress.'
Like tumuli they stand, a sign of death,
Hideous and full of rottenness within!
Yet all too small to hold the streams of horror
That from the boiling founts of evil spring.
Sepulchral monuments where are interred
Th' effete and festering products of misrule,
Hidden from day that they the less may grieve,
Or shock with ghastly front the aching sense.

Society demands such shall not be:
It will not have its wonted peace disturbed
By any startling impropriety:
Appearance must be saved: all ugly sights
And outward signs of hollowness must still
Be varnished o'er, until the ruin burst!

"Such is the bedlam thou art called to rule,
No easy task nor sinecure nor fair
Inheritance thy due.   Let imbeciles
Discuss the rights divine of Kings, thou art
Nor more nor less than nature's minister,
The fittest found, chosen by dreadful rite
And fiery ordeal, which thou hast passed
By courage, promptitude and martial skill;
For courage which is oft the surest pledge
Of innate kindness, intellect and worth
To lower natures is by Heaven denied
Or granted sparingly, proportional

To any good or virtue in them found.
Therefore assume the baton of command
Or what you will, the purple robe or crown;
The weight, no doubt, will gall thy laden brow;
But yet it is for common good of all,
Such good, at least, as men are fitted for.
Where rapine reigns and violence, or where
About to come, premonitory showing,
A King is the preventative and cure
Together joined, now, as in Israel old
When all the suffering people cried, oppressed
By Eli's and by Samuel's sons, give us
A king to rule us like the nations round.
For some one still the wayward multitude
Must have to look to and to idolize—
Some soldier knight whose innate strength of will
Shall save them from oppressors in their need.

"The reins of power thou art called to guide;

Thy office is for life; if thou relax
Thy grasp or steer awry, destruction waits.
Now, to thy place; the whip of justice ply
With vigor, and this rod of iron wield,
In mercy wield; lesson somewhat thereby
The sum inordinate of human woe;
The groaning millions, succor and restrain,
Protect man 'gainst himself, his greatest foe,
Nor grieve too much where imperfections reign
That things are not as perfect as they ought;
For evils necessarily will abound,
Do what thou wilt; thy office is the proof.
But bear in mind to keep thy temper well
Under the curb, or, like a restive steed,
'Twill drag thee hence to dangerous extremes;
For thou art head and guardian of the laws,
So indispensable or wherefore used,
The saviour, judge and minister combined,
To heal henceforth, restrain and rule mankind.

THE CONQUEROR'S DREAM.

He ceased, and straightway all grew dark as night,
And instantaneous there on every side,
Uprose intense, the clank of chains and clash
Of steel, the din of arms and tramp of horse,
Commingled all with the loud battle-cry
Of hosts uniting in the shock of war.
Low thunders moaned, reverberating wide :
Wave after wave of earthquake swept the land :
The mighty towers to their foundations swayed !
So dreadful was the noise and turmoil that
It seemed as if the end of things had come,
And ancient Night with Chaos reigned once more!
Then all again grew still, in silence hushed :
And in the East there dawned, uprising slow
A roseate blush, a tinge of golden light,
The herald sure of a more glorious morn,
A time of rest if not the reign foretold
Of peace on earth! and so the vision passed!

THE PALM GROVES.

In the dimming light of evening,

By the water's haunted margin,

Rise the palm groves grand and gloomy

Waving wierdly in the twilight,

Sighing sadly in the night-wind,

To the ocean's wail responding,

As they chant their lonely vespers

O'er the spectres and the shadows,

O'er the graves of the departed,

O'er the bones of the forgotten,

Bleaching bones that strew the sea-beach

From the faithless sands uplifted.*

* Groves alluded to are situated at Parel, some five or six miles distant from the city of Bombay. The adjoining beach has been used as a burying ground. And the bones, from time to time

Full of awe and full of sadness,
Is their moaning in the twilight
O'er the flitting ghosts and shadows,
O'er the human bones that whiten,
Wasting mould'ring on the sea-shore!

What a language in their waving!
What a history in their singing!
Tales of ages dim uncertain,
Long before the glacial epoch,
When uncouth primeval monsters
Wandered by the Arctic Ocean,
By the melancholy waters
In the forests of the Northland.

With a loud voice and prophetic,
Ere man was, they sang his coming,

exposed from the shifting and blowing of the sand, getting strewn along the shore, give the place, in the evening twilight, a peculiarly wierd and lonely aspect.

For for him were they created.
Now they sing the past and present :—
How they taught earth's infant races,
How they for their wants provided,
How they gave them in abundance
Cooling drink and food and shelter.

Lovely date palms bending downwards,
Proudly showed their tempting clusters,
Saying "Take them, they are for you,
For you only have we grown them."

Feathery cocoas, waving gently,
Pointed to their laden bosoms,
Pointed to their nuts and fibres,
Pointed to their sheathing network
Wrapt around them like a garment :
Hinted to them, " Do as we do,
Take our fibres, twist them neatly,

Work them into pliant cordage,
Work them into woven textures,
They will serve for many uses."

Then they told the secret also,
Where they kept their oils and sugars,
Where they kept their pleasant juices,
Where they kept their subtle essence ;
Told them how they should ferment it ;
Of the pleasures it would bring them,
Of the dangers that would follow :
How the good it would make better,
How the wise it would make wiser,
How the strong it would make stronger,
How the vile it would make viler,
How the fool 'twould make more foolish,
How the weak it would extinguish.

Thus the nations were instructed

In the rudiments of knowledge,
In the principles of progress.
But they sang in riddles darkly,
Sang in accents deep and thrilling,
From the vulgar crowd concealing,
To the chosen few revealing
Other secrets, greater, grander,—
Of a higher life hereafter,
Of the culture of the spirit,
Of the harmonies in nature
Of the source of strength and beauty,
Of deformity and weakness.

Slowly step by step advancing,
With their never failing bounty,
They arrested man's attention ;
Then their beauty dawned upon him,
Kindling on his waking senses,
Calling up new life within him,

Filling him with strange emotion,
Foretaste of the joys of heaven!

Straightway then in broken measures
With rude song he lisped their praises,
In new garbs his fancy dressed them;
Each in turn took life before him,
Life and sense and sex and motion,
And their flowing plumes he likened
Unto maiden's shining tresses.

In this fashion sang the minstrels
Of the beauty of the palm trees;
Of the arrowy palmyras
When the moonlight through them streameth,
When the stars above them gleameth
In the ebon vault of heaven;
Of the date's recumbent leafage
Rustling in the sultry noonday;

Of the cocoa's feathery plumage
Gently bending to the east wind,
Grandly swaying to the west wind,
Floating on the aerial currents,
Tossing in the winds of heaven;
Of the grandeur of their motion,
Of the magic of their singing,
Of their anthems deep and solemn
Rising, floating on the night-wind
Like the sound of distant waters,
Like æolian harps in motion
Breathing forth their mystic music,
Played upon by unseen fingers,
By the spirits of the ether!

Thus they sang in distant ages,
And thus sing they in the present.
In the sultry Indian climates,
In the shadow of pagodas,

THE PALM GROVES.

By the sacred groves and rivers
Still are heard the ancient measures,
Of the glory of the palm trees,
Of their beauty grace and splendor ;
How they lead their lives of pleasure,
Of munificence and pleasure,
Sporting with the winds of heaven,
With the am'rous winds of heaven !

So the palms of every genus
In the dawning of the ages
Were the friends and were the teachers
Of the infant race of mankind :
Ever vieing with each other,
Ever giving and bestowing,
Showering comforts on the people,
In the unrecorded epochs,
In the twilight of creation,
In the past more than the present,

For their urgent wants providing.

Thus they lead their lives of pleasure,
Lives of innocence and pleasure,
In the sunlight and the shadow,
In the dreamy sultry noontide,
In the haunted air of midnight,
In the soft and mystic moonlight;
Ever vieing with each other,
Ever wooing and caressing,
Ever singing, waving, sighing,
Sporting with the winds of heaven,
With the am'rous winds of heaven,
Till they each in time sink prostrate,
Shattered by the faithless lovers,
Till the whirlwinds in their anger,
Till the storm-winds in their fury,
Reeling, swaying with excitement
In their madness seize upon them;

Till the cyclone loud and boisterous,
Rushing, blindly in his passion,
With his rude and fierce caresses,
Snaps them through the slender middle,
Sweeps the cold earth with their tresses,
With their fair and flowing tresses,
And unheeding onward passes,
Sinking beauty in corruption,
Shrouding her in gloom and sadness,
Shrouding her in death and darkness;
In the darkness whence she issued,
Springing into light and morning,
Into momentary being,
Like a transient meteor flashing,
Flashing in the dark abysses,
In the depths of the unknown!

THE SOLDIERS' CEMETERY, KHANDALLA.

DID hand of genius select, or chance
Or wide controlling destiny decree
This fairest resting place of those that were?
The lone and frenzied poet, wand'ring 'midst
The waste and barren rocks of Caucasus,
Found not a grave 'mongst scenes so wild and grand
As those that lie around Khandalla's hill—
Encircled cemetery. The mould'ring forms
That now within its hallowed precincts sleep,
Were they once nature's gentle worshippers?
That thus before their silent tombs she spreads
With lavish hand her richest drapery!

On either side uneven mountains rise
In endless shapes, like jagged and broken walls,

And high embattled towers that o'erlook

The deep defiles and long extended vales.

Impervious forests clothe the dark ravines,

And stunted shrubs, the mountain's fissured sides;

And flowering creepers in profusion spread

And with their garlands drape the rocky heights.

Pure crystals streams of snowy whiteness rush

With ceaseless din adown the shattered rocks,

As though they sang eternal requiem

For ever by the exiles lonely graves;

While o'er them perched on yew or evergreen

The jetty whistler of the steep prolongs

His melancholy notes, solemn and sad,

Yet careless and resigned withal, as if

He recked not now or aught of sorrow knew.*

---

* The bird alluded to belongs to the thrush family, and is a variety or a nearly allied species to the common blackbird, which it resembles. It is intensely black, with a bluish tinge, well marked on the points of the shoulders. Its notes are plaintive and melancholy, and resemble greatly the persevering efforts of a boy learning to whistle; and on this account, no doubt, it is sometimes called the gentleman whistler. It is

SOLDIERS' CEMETERY, KHANDALLA.

While far beyond the misty hills that rise
At intervals like clouds against the sky
Spreads mirror-like the wide-encircling sea
Whose restless waters lap the distant shores
Of their loved island homes down in the west.
Its placid surface, bright as burnished gold,
Now sends the slanting beams of evening sun
Athwart the hills and rock-based cemetery,
Like rays of hope from fairer lands that know
Not death, bright harbingers that seem to say
Sleep on in peace ye silent forms, and trust
What yet for you kind nature has in store,
What yet for you will be evolved from out
The boundless ocean of eternity!"

heard chiefly during the rains, and is never seen far from the cliff or steep which it frequents. It is a shy bird and very difficult to see whilst it sings.

THE WARBLER AND THE BIRD-COLLECTOR.

Whilst cowering 'neath the shades of night
   Within a templed grove,
The trembling of its breast to still,
   A timid warbler strove.

The sacred place its life had given,
   But cruel fate did sever
From all life's joys from home and kin
   The tiny thing forever.

And homeless now, an outcast lone,
   Far hence on swift wings borne,
In distant lands its hapless lot
   The wanderer shall mourn.

Till now upon the stream of time,
    As on a crystal tide,
With loving mate, with kindred near,
    Its fragile form did glide.

Still, when the roseate blush of dawn,
    Suffused the vault of night,
Its early matins sweetly rang
    To greet the rising light.

E'en brooding Melancholy smiled,
    Infected by the spell,
That as from gushing fount of joy
    In glowing sparkles fell.

With song it lulled itself to rest
    When dewy eve drew near,
And misty twilight softly closed
    In folding shadows drear.

So went the happy hours along,
  Till like a withering blast,
His blighting glance athwart its course
  Creation's lord did cast.

Within the calm retreat he came,
  Soft music flowed around,
But quick through all the startled grove
  Is heard a ringing sound.

No tender pity touched his breast,
  Or his cold nature bent,
As to each unsuspecting bird
  The hissing lead he sent.

The little warbler wond'ring saw,
  Its comrades fall around,
Their fair forms soiled with trickling blood
  Cast helpless on the ground.

It wond'ring saw them one by one,
    Caught up with miser care;
The bird-collector took them hence,
    Away it knew not where.

Away to deck some thoughtless maid,
    Some vain, luxurious wife;
Or silent stand in gloomy hall,
    In mockery of life.*

And long it looked for their return,
    And called with plaintive note,
Yet nought but 'th echoes ghostly wail
    Upon the air did float,

But when exhausted with its cares,
    It sank in troubled sleep,
They seemed far on a journey lone
    Upon the trackless deep.

* See man a special creation (chapter IV, in defence of small birds.)

And then, anon, it seemed itself
   In dreary lands to stray,
Its loved and lost ones seeking still,
   In vain from day to day.

But soon as darkness shrank to west
   Before the orient light,
Led by the dream's illusive show,
   It bends its distant flight.

And swiftly cleaves the yielding air
   Along the track of day,
Till late above the ocean's waste
   It holds its lonely way.

And ah! where shall its course be stayed?
   No resting place is near,
But far ahead the waters spread,
   And crested waves appear.

A leaden hue o'ercasts the sky,
    And banking clouds arise ;
The billows frown beneath the shade
    That thickening o'er them lies.

And angry gusts alternate sigh
    Or chafe with rage suppressed,
Like chargers held upon the rein
    In line of battle dressed.

Till at the signal given they rush
    Resistless on the plain ;
So pause the winds a moment now
    Above the wintry main.

The inky clouds, the coming night,
    A dreary shadow cast,
Still through the gloom the wand'rer speeds
    Before the rising blast.

And now the storm descends amain,
    The giant billows leap
And toss aloft their hissing spray
    High o'er the yawning deep.

Then droop at length its weary wings
    In the unequal strife,
And lower sink, and lower still,
    As ebbs the stream of life.

But as it neared the fatal wave
    A ship's light gleamed ahead,
Then swift it upward shoots again,
    By sudden impulse led.

Through th' elemental war it swept,
    The reeling bark it gained,
Then sank exhausted on the deck,
    The springs of life o'erstrained.

One fearless form there stood amidst
    That dread commotion wild;
He thought then on his distant home,
    And on his orphan child.

He saw the bird before him drop;
    He took it up with care;
It was a little timid thing,
    Of radiant beauty rare.

He stroked it gently with his hand;
    A tear glanced in his eye;
But quick as vivid lightning shoots
    His grief and troubles fly.

It seemed to say "Be of good cheer,
    Nor fear the angry tide,
Remember now who calms the sea,
    And in His mercy bide.

Behold in me the sign He sends;
　Believe the token true;
He bore me from the boiling deep,
　And so shall now bear you."

The little harbinger he stowed
　In roomy cage away
Where food and drink in ample store
　Before it neatly lay.

Meanwhile the winds and waves abate;
　The laboring ship's o'erhauled;
The pumps are manned, the leak is found,
　And hope again recalled.

The broken spars are soon replaced;
　The sails again are spread;
And steadily before the breeze
　They onward bear ahead.

So speed they gaily on each day
    Until the port is gained,
Then eagerly they crowd on shore
    Till hardly one remained.

The master took his little charge
    Uninjured from the sea,
He took it to his daughter fair
    And told its history.

And much she wondered, much she wept;
    She wept for joy and fear;
The master kissed his loving child
    And dropped a silent tear.

And then they hasten on the lawn
    To set the captive free;
They long to see it on the wing
    Flitting from tree to tree.

Right joyously they saw it soar
   And vanish in the air ;
And then contentedly returned
   From true enacted prayer.

Would that the gentle warbler had
   Likewise a resting found ;
But it shall wander still, alas!
   The wilds far spread around.

And many a lonely steppe shall pass,
   And barren desert strange,
Or stray where the glacier slow doth creep
   Through many an Alpine range.

In vain seeking on earth forlorn
   The peace it ne'er shall find ;
For its home is where its loved ones rest,
   The home for it designed!

THE EYRIE ON THE SEA-CLIFF.

Part I.

Now the purple sun of morning
Shed his radiance o'er the landscape,
Rolled the white fog from the mountains,
Sipped the dew from off the grasses,
Quaffed the nectar from the flowers,
From the lowly, laughing flowers;
Called the minstrels of the woodland,
Called the linnets, larks and finches,
Forth to chant their early matins.

Proudly perched there on a pine tree,
Conscious of her vocal powers,
Leader of the choral songsters,
Sat a throstle blithely singing,

And the others sang responsive,
Till with song the air was flooded,
Till their music loud re-echoed
From each hollow rock and cranny
Through the undulating valley.

Here a sparrow-hawk drew near them;
Full of mischief was his bosom;
In his eye was evil lurking.
Said the thrush then rather angry,
"Keep your distance I command you;"
Straightway dropping, as she said so,
Down between the leafy branches,
Taking refuge 'mong the prickles,
For she did not like the glitter
Of his curious eyes upon her.

But the hawk began to wheedle,
And to swear upon his honor

That he merely meant to listen,
If she only would permit him;
Said his very soul was ravished
By the magic of her singing;
Said he loved her most sincerely,
Loved her long, and loved her dearly·
Praised her loudly for her beauty,
For her mottled heaving bosom,
And the sweetness of her singing,
Getting nearer as he did so,
Getting nearer still and nearer.

Then in this wise spake unto her:
"I can from all foes protect you:
From the chattering piebald magpie
Busy babbling ugly slander;
From the jackdaw, self important,
Cawing 'bout the laws of nature;
From the brooding raven yonder,

Croaking, ever discontented,
Hatching treason and sedition;
From the spectral owl that hooteth,
Gliding on his downy pinions
Nightly by the haunted ruins!"

This and much more said the falcon,
Said the subtle wily falcon
Growing bolder and more pressing.
Then in this wise he proceeded—
"Ah! what life and beauty wasted!
Buried here among the brambles,
'Mong those dark and tangled thickets;
Come now, come, and don't be silly:
Fly with me to yonder headland,
Yonder bold and jutting headland,
Looking proudly o'er the water,
O'er the restless, rolling water.
I have built me there a mansion,

Built me there a lordly mansion,
By the deep, resounding ocean.
You shall see the white ships sailing,
To and fro upon the water;
See the mermaids 'mong the green waves
Far below the rocky ramparts!
See the fays by moonlight tripping
To their weird enchanting music
Round the hawthorn near the fountain
By the green mound on the headland!"

And the silly thrush, like Eva,
Could not stand against temptation,
Could not grieve the heart that loved her:
And she came forth wondering, fearing,
Trembling like a leaf in spring time,
Making many resolutions,
Just to see him for an instant,
For a moment to be near him

And return within her thicket.

Broken were her resolutions,
When she heard his protestations;
And the silly thrush, like Eva,
Yielded to her wily tempter:
Longed to gain forbidden knowledge
Longed to cull the fruits of pleasure;
Could not stand against temptation.

Then the hawk began to chuckle,
As he hooked his talons round her;
Half entreating, half enforcing,
Half in jest and more in earnest,
Said he, " Let me now, my dearest,
Have the honor to escort you,"
As he bore her, unresisting,
To his eyrie on the sea-cliff,
To his stronghold on the headland.

Part II.

First the time passed very gaily
Through the pleasant months of summer,
For the hawk was all endearment,
All politeness and attention,
And she loved him very truly,
Wondered how she could e'er doubt him.

There beneath the castle windows,
In the sun the seals were basking,
In the water played the dolphins,
Rolling, tumbling, 'mong the billows,
On the wing the noisy sea-gulls
Clamored o'er the shoaling fishes,
Pitching headlong down among them ;
On the shelving rocks and ledges

THE EYRIE ON THE SEA-CLIFF.

Sat the divers and the guillemots,
And the silent brooding corm'rants.

All around her was enchanting,
Scenes of vastness and of grandeur
Burst upon her wond'ring senses.
There she saw the great Atlantic
Stretching far away to westward;
Saw the white ships sailing on it;
Saw the shining moonfield nightly
Trembling on its placid surface;
Saw the mermaids 'mong the green waves
Far below the rocky ramparts;
Heard the wild notes of their singing
Blending with the sounds of ocean;
Saw the fays by moonlight tripping
To their weird enchanting music
Round the hawthorn near the fountain
By the green mound on the headland!

But too swiftly fled the moments,
Fled those transient hours of pleasure,
Passing as a shadow passeth
'Neath a drifting cloud in autumn.

As the pleasant summer faded
And the storms of winter gathered
Cold and careless grew the falcon;
Day by day grew more estranged,
And at length became uncivil;
Muttered hoarsely his displeasure,
Gazed with frowning look upon her
And her spirit felt the shadow
Of some undefined disaster,
Of some fast approaching sorrow.
Thus the evil days came nigh her.
And the tempest closed upon her.

All was changed around the headland,

In the very air was sadness;
Far the sun to south receded,
And the vapors spread to northward
Like a curtain o'er the heavens.
Loudly moaned the surging billows;
Dark and dismal grew the ocean;
Vanished were the white ships from it;
Vanished too the fays and mermaids;
And she only saw the Banshee
Nightly by the troubled water;
Only heard the Banshee's wailing
And the shrieking of the storm fiend;
Only heard the wail of sorrow,
Heard the plaintive wail of sorrow
And the boding cry of anguish
Ringing from the haunted caverns.
And she trembled like an aspen,
Like an aspen leaf in autumn;
And she could not still the beating,

Could not still the heavy beating,
Of her troubled heart within her;
And she prayed the hawk to send her
To her old home in the woodland
With imploring look and language
With unutterable longing!

But the hawk still dark and sullen
Spoke with rude, disdainful accent;
Raised his wings with angry gesture,
Looked with baleful eyes upon her.

Here her lingering hope now vanished,
Here the darkness closed around her,
And no ray of light came nigh her,
Came to guide her or restrain her:
And her spirit quailed with terror,
Quailed beneath the ghastly promptings
Of the demons that beset her

Till her reason reeled and tottered,
Till she rushed upon the ramparts
Overcome with pain and sorrow;
Wildly rushed upon the ramparts
That o'erlooked the hissing water;
Sought the jutting ledge's margin;
Looked beneath her, paused and shuddered;
Raised her eyes and stumbled forward,
Falling with a cry of anguish,
With a stifled cry of anguish
That her life-blood seemed to curdle
And her being seemed to shatter.
Soon were ended all her sorrows
Ended too her transient pleasures;
Like a rose culled in the budding,
Bloomed a moment, drooped and withered.
Morning saw some tufted feathers,
Saw some soiled and tufted feathers
Tossed about the stormy headland;

And no more now sang the throstle
In her woodland home forever!

THE HEIGHTS OF KHANDALLA.

HIGH seated 'mong the hills, Khandalla lies
'Mid scenes such as a dreamer sees at times
Unfolded in the silence of the night
When slumber on the waking sense doth fall.
On either hand far as the eye can reach
Plains, rivers, seas, forests and mountains spread.
Around, at intervals, fair nestling vales,
Freely traversed by light-reflecting streams,
And decked with many a green and shady grove,
Beneath their rugged walls securely lie.
But how describe the indescribable!
Or paint in words the grandeur of the scene!
There jagged and gloomy mountains rise abrupt,
Crowned with deceptive and fantastic shapes

THE HEIGHTS OF KHANDALLA.

Of giant forts, of spires and domes and towers
And mighty keeps and wide enchanted halls,
Where legends say the mountain demons dwell.
Stupendous frowning peaks uplift on high
Their hoary summits lightning scathed and bare
Like sentinels that keep eternal watch
Far o'er the silent and secluded glens
That wind beneath their walls of adamant.
Hoar sentinels, against whose stalwart sides
The wasting shocks of circling periods roll.
The types of perpetuity they stand,
And strength, majestic wonder-moving forms,
From age to age alike unchanged, mid change.
The same when their colossal summits blot,
With outline clear, the azure sky of day,
As when in twilight shades they vaguely loom,
And stand like clouds above the shifting mists,
Obscure and vast as in a passing dream;
Or when in blackest night the lightning's flash,

With sudden glare, the blinding gloom dispels,
Disclosing there in momentary light
Rocks, caves and ravines, gulfs and gaping chasms.
But now in darkness clad, as with a pall
Thick robed, against the tempest's rage they stand,
Witnessing there the elemental strife
With all the horrors that the time calls forth;
For now, by need and ravening hunger pressed,
The fearful denizens of the waste take up
Their nightly vigils and accustomed rounds.
There in the narrow pass the gaunt snake rolled
In horrid folds terrible as death keeps watch,
Intent with quick unerring dart to seize
And bind in deadly coils, as in a vice,
The unsuspecting brute that wanders near
Unmindful of the hidden foe. Here too
The tiger stalks, cat-like with stealthy pace,
In search of prey, and all the lesser tribes,
Now singly, now in packs united, hunt,

THE HEIGHTS OF KHANDALLA.

Or o'er the carcass of some fallen beast
Or corse exhumed, hold carnival accurst,
Startling the night with hideous laugh the while *
Or savage growl or piercing ghoul-like cry.
Among the hills, in broken masses piled,
The storm-clouds drive before the wintry gusts
Till sponge-like pressed against the mountain's sides,
And by fierce lightning riven, whole floods they send
From ledge to ledge adown the rocky steeps,
Rushing as from an aerial reservoir.
And still the tempest raves; with hideous crash
The loosened cliffs, precipitous, descend
With ruin fraught, thund'ring into the vale ! †
The whirlwinds reel around the jutting crags,
And storm sprites moan within the haunted caves,

* Hyenes are noted in India for their horrible laughter, and the jackalls for their weird and unearthly cries.

† Such falls of rocks and cliffs are common among the hills, but are only heard of where they occasion great loss of life and property, as at Khandalla in 1875, and lately at Naini Tal in the northwest of Bengal.

The lone and dismal wailings blending oft
With fearful cries and wild discordant yells,
With ghostly echoes and unearthly sounds,
The hoarse and hollow roar of tumbling torrents
And crashing din of thunder intermingled.
Dread awe-inspiring harmonies of discord,—
Terror and grandeur with each other blent
Beyond the power of artist to portray.
Fit emblem of the passing storms that beat
In hours of darkness round the human soul,
The gloomy doubts and promptings of despair,
The horrid phantoms that in dread array
On every side with fiercest rage assail
Until the rising beams of light that spring
From reason, hope and childlike trust dispel
The monstrous brood that flap on demon wings
Like harpies from the stygian pool uprisen.
So too the earthly scenes revolve and pass;
Night's rushing storms and grizzly spectres flee

Before the brightness of the orient sun.
Unchanged in aught the mighty hills uplift
Their rugged heights and towering peaks to heaven.
How different now the harmonies that blend
To greet the morn beneath their passive forms!
The opening flowers unfold their hidden charms
And wide diffuse celestial odors round.
The warblings of a thousand tongues are heard,
For now the gentle denizens of the air
Come forth to chant their wonted hymns of praise,
And wake the fount of rapture till the earth
Seems glad and sympathizing nature smiles!

BY THE SAME AUTHOR.

THE
CAUSE OF COLOR AMONG RACES,
AND THE
EVOLUTION OF PHYSICAL BEAUTY.

"Dr. W. Sharpe, whose poetical works are pretty well known, has reprinted in a neat little book some highly interesting and suggestive remarks on the cause of color among races, and the evolution of physical beauty. . . . This is a subject which hitherto has been almost wholly neglected though affording a wide field for profitable and instructive research."—*Graphic.*

"Dr. Sharpe, who is favorably known as the author of two volumes of poems of great merit, has just issued a remarkably interesting little volume discussing the cause of color among races, and the evolution of physical beauty. . . . It is impossible to do more than give an outline of Dr. Sharpe's conclusions, but those who are interested in the subject will do well to examine them in detail in his closely reasoned and signally able volume."—*Birmingham Daily Gazette.*

"Both these subjects are of interest, and they are treated in an able manner by the author, who is known as an original thinker and graceful writer."—*Peterborough Advertiser.*

"He also brings out clearly the important effects of habit and occupation upon the mind and body, and the mighty influence of heredity in moulding the character of successive generations."—*Dublin Mail.*

"Dr. Sharpe's reasoning is clear and his points well chosen. To those interested in the subject of ethnology we especially commend his thoughtful little work, believing that it will prove not only interesting but instructive."—*New York Daily Graphic*

"As Ethnology has recently received great attention, it is a seasonable contribution to the discussion of that matter-of-fact state of things which exists in this world of ours."—*Freemason.*

"The same benevolent ideas pervade Dr. Sharpe's other works, especially 'The Cause of Color among Races, and the Evolution of Physical Beauty.' His opinions have not been hastily formed, and he advances many curious and interesting facts in support of them. His theory is, that not only physiognomy is affected by the indulgence of the lower passions, but that the nature of races may become so debased and brutalized in the course of ages that their very color becomes affected. . . . Of this he gives some remarkable instances, and certainly proves by the instance of Jews settled for centuries in India, that climate alone will not account for the problem."—*Social Notes.*

"The writer supports his theory with much fact and not a little clever argument; and these pages should be read by all who feel any interest on the subject whether viewed from a scientific or religious point of view."—*Brief.*

"This is one of the smallest, thinnest and most curious of little books."—*Illustrated Sporting and Dramatic News.*

"Incidentally these pages are enriched with really eloquent denunciation of the evils which abound in our social state."—*Nonconformist.*

"Has the merit of sincere conviction and of a graceful style. His prose is as good as his poetry."—*Public Opinion.*

"In this little volume Dr. Sharpe puts forth some views about the cause of color which are well worth studying."—*Broad Arrow.*

"A short but interesting essay, in which the author lays it down that the tendency of the color of man is from dark to light as races become more and more civilized."—*Land and Water.*

London Publisher, DAVID BOGUE, 3 St. Martin's Pl., W. C.

THE CONQUEROR'S DREAM
AND OTHER POEMS.

PRESS NOTICES.

"THE above work, though unpretentious in length, deserves special attention on account of the true poetic feeling evinced in its composition. . . . Lofty sentiment and graceful diction characterize it throughout, but they are particularly noticeable in the poem which gives its name to the collection and which is written in blank verse, the most elevated of all measures, and at the same time the most difficult to succeed in, since a correct ear, a delicate taste, and true poetical genius are essential to its perfect development. Dr. Sharpe has proven himself to be in a great degree master of this effective but not easy method of versification. . . . There are many truths conveyed in the reading of this poem, and the conclusions reached are those of a thoughtful and far-seeing mind. Dr. Sharpe has, besides the qualities we have already enumerated, the clever faculty of never wearying his reader; what he says he utters delicately and expressively, but never at too great length. His thought is vigorous, his language well chosen, and the result is that what he writes is well worthy of attention, and will repay perusal."—*New York Daily Graphic*.

"Dr. Sharpe writes most musically, and his poem on the Palm Groves is perfect as far as it goes. It is modelled, of course, on Mr. Longfellow's 'Hiawatha,' the rhythm of which in itself is most attractive, and Dr. Sharpe has put an exquisite picture upon the model. We cannot refrain from quoting a final passage."—*Lloyd's Weekly News*.

"The six poems comprised in the little book before us are marked with a loftiness of sentiment and care of finish which should render them acceptable to the most cultivated taste. That the author is a devout worshipper in nature's temple is abundantly shown on every page; and it must be added that his inspiration is seconded by that scholarly instinct which rejects alike the commonplace and the extravagant. The chief composition, 'The Conqueror's Dream,' is an admirable and powerful poem in blank verse, and withal designed to convey a useful lesson. More freedom is, however, displayed in the shorter pieces, several of which, as 'The Palm Groves' and

'The Warbler and the Bird Collector,' have the characteristics of veritable gems of verse."—*Birmingham Daily Gazette.*

"Some of the minor pieces, such as 'The Warbler and the Bird Collector,' are especially pleasing, possessing as they do almost Wordsworthian simplicity and beauty."—*Literary World.*

"Of these poems the 'Conqueror's Dream' claims undoubted precedence."—*Modern Thought.*

"Those who enter upon its perusal will find themselves well repaid for the time so spent."—*City Press.*

"We are glad to mention approvingly the little book."—*Freemason.*

"These poems show that the author is gifted with true poetic feeling, while his blank verse — a somewhat rare accomplishment—is flowing and melodious."—*Broad Arrow.*

"We cordially recommend these pages as eminently calculated to delight, being natural, fresh and charming."—*Metropolitan.*

"The poem called 'The Palm Groves' is full of weird pictures of the groves near Bombay, where the beach is strewn with human bones."—*Academy.*

"The work is a little treasure for those who know how to appreciate a cultivated imagination and elegantly expressed sentiments and ideas."—*Western Daily Mercury.*

"The metres are good and musical, especially the blank verse, which is always a good sign; and the imagination displayed in the reproduction of Indian scenery is of a high order. But really the best thing in the book is the allegorical description, in the first poem, of the tower which signifies the Summit of Ambition, especially the passage on the loneliness of fame."—*Graphic.*

"'The Conqueror's Dream' is a poem of considerable length in blank verse. It presents many vivid and highly poetical fancies, not unusually of a highly poetical imagination. The picture of bodily suffering so true to the life of men with 'shrivelled faces and their hollow eyes' could have been written only by a physician who is also a bard to boot. We must especially call attention to 'The Palm Groves' and 'The Warbler and the Bird Collector,' which are simple and touching poems of no ordinary merit."—*Public Opinion.*

London Publisher, DAVID BOGUE 3 St. Martin's Pl., W. C.

www.ingramcontent.com/pod-product-compliance
Lightning Source LLC
Chambersburg PA
CBHW020227090426
42735CB00010B/1607